rounds

Rounds is a series of circular characters whose real-life stories start where they end which is why they are called

rounds

Rounds is a series of circular characters whose real-life stories start where they end which is why they are called

To our mums and
dads, with love

First published 2016 by Nosy Crow Ltd
The Crow's Nest, 10a Lant Street
London SE1 1QR
www.nosycrow.com

ISBN 978 0 85763 697 3 (HB)
ISBN 978 0 85763 698 0 (PB)

Nosy Crow and associated logos are trademarks
and/or registered trademarks of Nosy Crow Ltd.

Concept and story research by Barry Tranter and Emma Tranter
Text © Emma Tranter 2016
Illustrations © Barry Tranter 2016
Consultant: Chris Jarvis, Education Officer at the Oxford University Museum of Natural History

The right of Emma Tranter to be identified as the author and Barry Tranter
to be identified as the illustrator of this work has been asserted.

A CIP catalogue record for this book is available from the British Library.

Printed in China by Imago

Papers used by Nosy Crow are made
from wood grown in sustainable forests.

1 3 5 7 9 8 6 4 2 (HB)
1 3 5 7 9 8 6 4 2 (PB)

# Parker Penguin

Let's dive in!

Barry Tranter

nosy crow

Emma Tranter

Antarctica is covered in ice. Lumps of ice that break off and float in the sea are called icebergs.

Antarctica is the coldest, driest and windiest place in the world.

Meet Parker. Parker is a penguin.
Here he is in the freezing cold and ice
of Antarctica, near the South Pole.

Hello, I'm Parker.
Nice to meet you!

Parker is an emperor penguin, the largest type of penguin in the world.

Parker is just a young penguin – he still has some growing to do!

Penguins have fatty bodies and four layers of feathers to keep them warm.

Although Parker is a bird, he can't fly. So he does a lot of walking instead. He can walk for miles and miles.

I keep trying but I just can't fly!

Penguins have small wings called flippers.

Left, right, waddle, waddle.

Because they have short legs, penguins waddle from side to side when they walk.

Waddling doesn't use much energy so penguins can walk a very long way.

But that's not the only way Parker gets around – he loves to slide on his front, too. It's much quicker than waddling!

Penguins push themselves along using their flippers and feet.

Wheeee!

Sliding on the ice like this is called tobogganing.

Parker is an excellent swimmer and spends most of his time in the water. He dives into the sea with a big splash!

Penguins make a special oil to keep their feathers waterproof.

Under the water, Parker is very graceful. He uses his flippers to speed along.

Penguins can't breathe underwater but they can hold their breath for up to 20 minutes!

Icebergs are mostly under the water – only their tips poke up above the surface.

Look at me go!

When they swim, penguins use their webbed feet to steer themselves.

Parker finds all his food in the sea. He eats fish and other sea creatures, such as squid and tiny shrimp-like animals called krill.

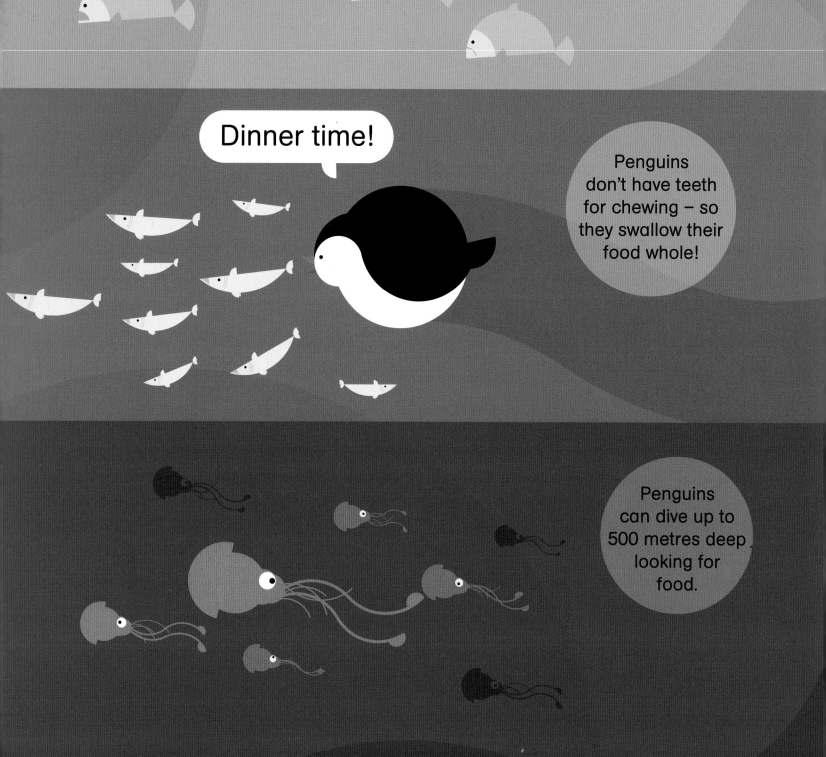

Dinner time!

Penguins don't have teeth for chewing – so they swallow their food whole!

Penguins can dive up to 500 metres deep, looking for food.

Penguins are carnivores, which means they eat other creatures but do not eat plants.

Their strong beaks and rough tongues help penguins to catch slippery fish.

Penguins have excellent eyesight which helps them to find food underwater.

Watch out, Parker! Bigger animals hunt for food, too. Killer whales and leopard seals lurk under the water, waiting for their chance to eat a penguin!

Uh oh!

Penguins swim quickly to escape danger, but the safest place is up on the ice.

Killer whales are also called orcas.

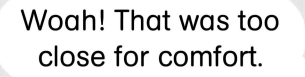

Woah! That was too close for comfort.

Penguins can jump up to two metres out of the water, onto the ice.

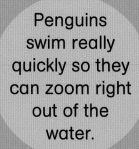

Penguins swim really quickly so they can zoom right out of the water.

Leopard seals have spotted coats like a leopard.

As Parker gets older, he grows taller and taller. By the time he is three years old he is fully-grown.

When penguins change their feathers, this is called moulting.

Now Parker is fully-grown, he's ready to find a mate. And he's not the only one on the lookout for a female!

Penguins are ready to start mating when they are four years old.

Many penguins return to the place where they were born to find a mate.

Emperor penguins are the only animal to spend the winter in Antarctica.

At the start of the winter, he joins lots and lots of penguins as they march to their breeding ground, where the females will lay their eggs.

I hope I meet a nice female penguin!

Penguins walk up to 75 miles to their breeding grounds.

# At last, Parker arrives at the breeding ground. There are lots of penguins here.

Emperor penguins stay with the same mate for life!

Penguins usually breed in large groups so they can all watch out for danger.

As penguins dance, they learn their mate's voice. This will help them find each other again.

Parker calls out to attract a female penguin.
Soon he meets Penelope and they do
a special dance together.

Two months later, Penelope lays one precious egg. She passes it straight to Parker, then sets off on a long journey to the sea to look for food.

I'll keep our egg nice and warm until it hatches.

See you soon!

If the egg touches the ice it will freeze! Penguin parents must be very careful.

Parker balances the egg on his feet, tucked under his tummy feathers.

Parker looks after the egg through icy winds . . .

heavy snowfall . . .

and freezing rain.

The male penguins all huddle together for warmth.

About 70 days later, snug and warm on Parker's feet, the egg starts to hatch. A tiny, fluffy chick comes out.

Hello, little one.

In the middle of winter it is dark all day long in Antarctica.

It can take two or three days for a chick to hatch.

Soon Penelope is on her way back from the sea.
Parker and the chick call to her so she can find them.

Squaawk!

Penguins' calls can be heard from very far away.

Each penguin's call is different. This helps Penelope to recognise her family.

Squaawk!

Muuuummy!!

Penguin chicks are covered in soft baby feathers called down.

Now Penelope is back home, she feeds her chick
with the food she has gathered during her trip.

Penguins
need to watch
out for birds
like skuas that
like to eat
chicks.

When female
penguins bring
up food from
their tummies,
it is called
regurgitation.

About five months later, the chick
starts to lose his fluffy baby feathers.

Meet Percy, Parker's son. Percy is a penguin.
Here he is in the freezing cold and ice
of Antarctica, near the South Pole.

Hello, I'm Percy.
Nice to meet you!

All penguins
live near the
sea, in the
southern half
of the world.

Some types
of penguin live
in warm places,
such as Australia
and South
Africa.

There are
17 types of
penguin in
the world.

# The life cycle of a penguin

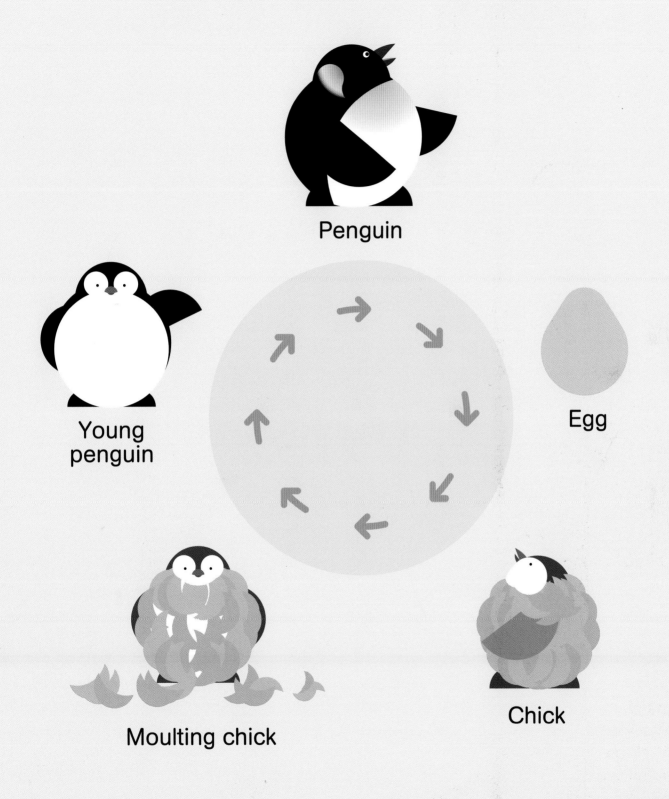

Penguin

Young penguin

Egg

Moulting chick

Chick

rounds

Rounds is a series of circular characters whose real-life stories start where they end which is why they are called Rounds is a series of circular characters whose real-life stories start where they end which is why they are called

rounds

Rounds is a series of circular characters whose real-life stories start where they end which is why they are called